T0147002

# For the Love of Me

## Parenting with Intention

# JJ CAMPAGNA

**BALBOA.**
PRESS

A DIVISION OF HAY HOUSE

Balboa Press books may be ordered through booksellers or by contacting:

Balboa Press
A Division of Hay House
1663 Liberty Drive
Bloomington, IN 47403
www.balboapress.com
1 (877) 407-4847

Print information available on the last page.

ISBN: 978-1-9822-1356-5 (sc)
ISBN: 978-1-9822-1357-2 (e)

Balboa Press rev. date:  10/03/2018

TO:

FROM:

DATE:

# Dedication

Dedicated to my two children,
six step children and nineteen
grandchildren who bless my life.

Through the years I have taken
my magic wand and instilled
the words of this book into the
heart and soul of each of you.

Your personalities are as varied
as the snowflakes drifting
across my window pane.

Each of you important, each needing
love, nurturing and guidance.

You make me proud!

I present to you my book
"For the Love of Me."

(Parenting with Intention)

One of life's unexpected pleasures:
children and grandchildren.

You make my "spirit" come
alive and bring joy to my heart.
You bring me full circle.

I now take pen in hand and
ask for guidance.

The seeds sown of yesterday are
our blessings of tomorrow!

I treasure the words given to
me as I write this keepsake:

It is written with guidance from above!

It is written for anyone who
touches the life of a child!

## "The Cloak of Responsibility"

When we become a parent we
take on a responsibility like none
we have ever experienced!

We are presented a little life
to "guide" and "nurture".

These precious little beings
depend on us for everything!

Being a parent is much more than
feeding a child, keeping it warm and
changing its diapers every few hours.

The intent we put into our children
in their childhood helps them to grow
into loving and truthful adults!

It is our duty to "guide and "direct"
them, to "teach" them love.

They learn love by example, by
seeing and feeling the warmth
of a close knit family.

They learn "self esteem" by having
a loving parent giving them positive
feedback and praise daily!

They learn to be caring
by being cared for.

They learn structure from living
within safe boundaries that you
provide; a united family working
together to "provide" as well as "teach"
strength and to understand failure.

I once read: A child cannot be allowed
to lie without consequences.

If no consequences are provided, he or
she shall never know "truthfulness."

I believe a child needs to feel
they are in a "secure" and
"safe" family environment.

If one's home is not provided with
safety how does he or she know what
is acceptable and unacceptable?

Rules must be "taught" and "applied!"

If a child is not provided with the
"knowledge" of a "safe" home how
does one's child know how to feel
secure in an unsafe world?

How will they know to teach
their offspring?

As parents, our true "traits"
come through our daily lives.

"Honesty," "truths" and "integrity"
are things children learn from us
by living these traits "daily."

Lives lived with grace and ease flow
through our offspring veins if we
have done our jobs correctly!

We are their example,
never forget that!

When one takes on parenthood one
takes on a huge "responsibility"!

Parenthood is a huge undertaking!

Parenthood is a huge sacrifice
on the part of "each" parent.

In our fast food lives of today we are
not making memories of the "Mother"
in the kitchen with the aroma of
fresh baked cookies coming from the
oven, the delight in a child's eyes as
they stir the dough, lick the spoon!

Yes, there is a mess to clean up, but you're making memories for them.

Allow children to make presents, they don't always have to buy things!

"Time" and "effort" show love!

It teaches patience. It teaches confidence.

It teaches them pride in their "accomplishments"!

In today's "whirlwind" lifestyle of working parents, birthday parties, dental and doctor appointments, and after school activities, children lose their sense of wonder.

We as parents need them to grow slowly not push them into growing up so fast!

They just spin and twirl into another day, another week, another month, another year!

Years go by and what have these little "beings", these little "joys" learned from you?

What have they taught you?

Do you read to them?

Do you have family meals together?

Along with "grace" being said every meal, perhaps you can try going around the table and say what each adult and child is thankful for!

Introduce other things into their thought process.

I am thankful for my friend "Joey".

Plant the "seeds" while they are small and as young adults see all your effort spring forth!

You are their lifelines to what they are going to be as they mature!

You are their role model!

You are their hero!

You are their example!

As a Mother of two, a step-mother to six and a grandparent to nineteen,

I find I use these teaching tools over and over again!

They are tried and true!

Plant the seeds of love and light to guide a child's way.

Seeds planted early take root as they grow into teenage years and on to young adulthood.

Water them with nurturing love.

Feed them daily with the miracle grow of words from this book.

Prune them in the direction they should go....but most of all be a true "example" for them to follow!

Nothing is as important as the "heart" and mind" of a child!

Please read this book through the years, again and again!

I thank you.

The children will thank you.

If you love me you will allow me
the gift of play and imagination!

Please do not hurry me
through my childhood.

Allow me to enjoy it! Enjoy it with me!

If you love me you will teach me
the joy of reading, by reading
to me as a small child.

If you love me teach me
boundaries at a young age.

If you love me you will honor my free will, but you will also teach me to understand the value of the word "No."

If you love me you will instill in me early in life the concept of "caring" and to respect another's feelings.

If you love me, set an example.

Do not lie for me. Children
learn by observing a parent.

They are very observant
and miss nothing!

"Children learn what they live."

If you love me you will give me time
instead of a mountain of toys.

Toys break and are tossed away.

Time given a child will make
wonderful memories.

A favorite story read aloud.

Laughs and giggles...
unforgettable memories.

If you love me you will teach me
the meaning and value of "truth"
so that I may stand proudly in
my own truths someday.

If you love me you will teach
me what honesty is.

You will teach me that little
white lies do count!

They lead to half truths
and omissions of truth.

If you love me you will teach me how to be a good loser as well as a good winner!

Both are so important!

If you love me you will put structure in my life, a framework that will help me all through my life's journey.

If you love me, teach me to be
courteous, to show politeness
and respect for others.

If you love me you will
teach me discipline.

You will chastise me when needed.

You will teach me of obedience.

If you love me you will teach me how to apologize and the meaning of "I am sorry."

If you love me you will teach me to awake daily with a song in my heart.

Please help me to understand what joy is.

If you love me you will teach
me respect for others as well
as respect for myself.

You will teach me respect for my toys,
my books as well as another's property.

If I am taught respect at a young age,
I shall carry this through my life.

If you love me you will teach me to love myself, which creates self-esteem.

If you love me, you will teach me
that tears are good for the soul.

If you love me you will teach
me to live with integrity.

If you love me you will teach me tolerance as well as kindness.

If you love me you will teach
me the art of listening.

If you listen to me, you will teach
me that my thoughts are valued.

If you love me you will teach
me to handle my "emotions" of
anger and disappointment.

You will teach me by "example"!

If you love me you will teach me to dream, but to always understand what reality is.

If you love me you will teach
me of nature, the sky, the sea
and the very air I breathe.

If you love me, you will provide for me a nurturing shelter, a space called home!

If you love me you will create a home that's secure, where harmony abides.

If you love me you will allow
music early in my life.

If you love me you will teach me of God
and that God is in each and everyone.

If you love me you will teach me to pray and to understand the value and power of prayer.

If you love me you will teach me
that beauty comes from within.

If you love me you will teach
me the value of family.

You will teach me to understand
the challenges of a family as
well as its joys and sorrows.

If you love me you will teach me of
friendships and how to be a friend.

Please teach me to choose
my friends wisely.

If you love me you will teach me that happiness cannot be bought or given to you; you create your own happiness.

If you love me you will teach
me of "contentment."

It is a state of happiness and being
satisfied with what one has.

If you love me you will teach
me to have respect for others
and to respect myself.

If you love me you will teach
me what Dignity is.

If you love me you will
teach me we are Love.

If you love me you will teach me the value of money and how to use it.

If you love me you will teach me of accountability and to be a responsible person.

If you love me you will teach me
of compassion for the elderly, the
less fortunate and for those that
are challenged in this lifetime.

If you love me you will teach me
that laughter lightens one's soul.

Please teach me that at certain times in
life on must learn to laugh at oneself!

If you love me you will
teach me empathy.

If you love me you will teach
me about life's choices and
consequences of wrong choices.

If you love me you will teach me to go inward to find right answers and to never be afraid to ask for help.

If you love me you will teach me the value of breath and that stillness and silence teach us much.

If you love me you will teach me as I grow that adversities are stepping stones of life and when we fail we can start anew.

If you love me you will teach me appreciation and to be thankful.

If you love me you will teach me
to admit when I am wrong.

It helps build relationships in later life.

If you love me please teach me of compassion and to be understanding.

If you love me you will teach me
of patience and how it can be
of use to me all through life.

If you love me please teach me
the art of being flexible.

If you love me you will teach me the art of problem solving at a young age.

If you step in and handle "all" my problems I will not learn to handle life's problems on my own.

If you love me you will teach me I am responsible for my actions and my words!

If you love me you will give me quality time, for time invested in me is so important!

If you love me you will teach me:

I have value!

I am important!

I am loved!

I am protected!

I am respected!

If you love me you will teach me what gratitude is.

Teach me to be appreciative and thankful.

Teach me to express it!

If you love me you will teach me the gift of sharing and to help others.

If you love me you will teach me
that everyone has a purpose
and a mission in this lifetime.

If you love me you will teach me the value of study and the "importance" of education.

If you love me you will teach me
we cannot all be leaders.

Some have to be followers, but to
follow only if it's in the right direction!

If you love me you will teach me to "accept" disappointments in life, as well as accomplishments.

If you love me please teach me
the attributes of developing
great character.

You will teach me by example.

You will make me proud
of our family name.

If you love me you will
teach me perseverance and
motivation by example

If you love me please teach me the meaning of modesty, to be decent in thoughts and actions.

If you love me please raise me to be a functional and morally conscious child.

If you love me you will teach
me the value of rules:

Parental rules

House rules

Life's rules

Please teach me it is not
just a "me" world.

If you love me please teach
me the art of forgiveness.

It will help me in my
journey through life.

Teach me to forgive myself
as well as others.

If you love me teach me of
loyalty and dependability.

If you love me please work with me and teach me how to conquer fear or despair, then I will know courage.

If you love me as I grow, allow me to innovate and create.

Please allow new ideas and new methods to flow through my brain.

Allow me to think.

Allow time to converse my opinions with you.

If you love me as an adolescent
teach me to filter my words.

Teach me to think before I speak.

If you love me teach me to be ethical.

Teach me to be someone who is honest
and follows good moral standards.

Teach me to be truthful,
fair and honest!

I believe ethics help determine
one's real value in this world

If you love me, you will teach
me all of the above.

By the time I reach adolescence,

I will then know how to be free
spirited and yet understand
humility and above all LOVE.

And of most importance:

If you love me you will
teach me by example!

Change in the world begins one person
at a time, one family at a time.

If you plant these seeds of wisdom in me, then I shall be able to also plant them in my future offspring.

## Watering the Lilies

Loved ones in our lives
are so important...

the love we give our children,
grandchildren, nieces, nephews and
neighborhood children helps them grow.

It's like watering the lilies in the
garden; the work you put into
them this year...blooms later...

The value of all your efforts
comes forth later as the flower
blooms the following year or
future years from now.

Love never goes "unnoticed."

The love you give is never
wasted...it's always of "value."

Some may be oblivious to it.

It may go right over their heads,
but in time, you receive the

reward of the effort given, time spent...it's never wasted.

Never forget to water your garden...your "loved ones."

As a parent we need to learn to bend and sway like the willow tree.

Be flexible, for life is full of adversities, learn from each one!

Delays and detours do appear, but so do unexpected pleasures and sweet surprises!

All are a part of life's earth journey.

Hang on and enjoy the ride!

Till we meet in person or on the printed page,

"Namaste."

Printed in the United States
By Bookmasters